A Note to Parents

DK READERS is a compelling program for beginning readers, designed in conjunction with leading literacy experts, including Dr. Linda Gambrell, Distinguished Professor of Education at Clemson University. Dr. Gambrell has served as President of the National Reading Conference, the College Reading Association, and the International Reading Association.

Beautiful illustrations and superb full-color photographs combine with engaging, easy-to-read stories to offer a fresh approach to each subject in the series. Each DK READER is guaranteed to capture a child's interest while developing his or her reading skills, general knowledge, and love of reading.

The five levels of DK READERS are aimed at different reading abilities, enabling you to choose the books that are exactly right for your child:

Pre-level 1: Learning to read
Level 1: Beginning to read
Level 2: Beginning to read alone
Level 3: Reading alone
Level 4: Proficient readers

The "normal" age at which a child begins to read can be anywhere from three to eight years old. Adult participation through the lower levels is very helpful for providing encouragement, discussing storylines, and sounding out unfamiliar words.

No matter which level you select, you can be sure that you are helping your child learn to read, then read to learn!

LONDON, NEW YORK, MUNICH,
MELBOURNE, and DELHI

DK LONDON
Series Editor Deborah Lock
US Senior Editor Shannon Beatty
Project Art Editor Ann Cannigs
Producer, Pre-production Francesca Wardell

Reading Consultant
Linda Gambrell, Ph.D.

DK DELHI
Editor Nandini Gupta
Art Editor Jyotsna Julka
DTP Designer Sachin Gupta
Picture Researcher Aditya Katyal
Deputy Managing Editor Soma B. Chowdhury

First American Edition, 2014
Published in the United States by DK Publishing
345 Hudson Street, New York, New York 10014

14 15 16 17 18 10 9 8 7 6 5 4 3 2 1
001—253409—August/14

A catalog record for this book is available
from the Library of Congress.

ISBN: 978-1-4654-1995-8 (Paperback)
ISBN: 978-1-4654-1994-1 (Hardcover)

DK books are available at special discounts when
purchased in bulk for sales promotions, premiums,
fund-raising, or educational use.
For details, contact:
DK Publishing Special Markets
345 Hudson Street, New York, New York 10014
SpecialSales@dk.com

Printed and bound in China by
South China Printing Company

The publisher would like to thank the following for
their kind permission to reproduce their photographs:
(Key: a=above, b=below/bottom, c=center, l=left, r=right, t=top)
3 Fotolia: Eric Isselee (clb). 4 Alamy Images: Maximilian Weinzierl (c).
Dreamstime.com: Kaarsten (c/torn paper). 5 Dorling Kindersley: Jerry
Young (t). Getty Images: Art Wolfe (tr). 8 Dreamstime.com: Kaarsten
(bl/torn paper). 9 Corbis: Frank Lane Picture Agency / Ron Austing (bc).
10–11 Corbis: Ch'ien Lee (b). 12–13 Alamy Images: Ernie Janes.
15 Alamy Images: Fotofeeling / Westend61 GmbH.
16 Corbis: SHOSEI (b). 19 Dreamstime.com: Paolo Pagani (tr).
20–21 Corbis: Minden Pictures / Mark Moffett. 22–23 Alamy Images:
Gian Luca Dedola. 24 Alamy Images: FLPA (t). 25 Science Photo
Library: Dr Morley Read (b). 26 Alamy Images: Carrie Garcia (t).
27 Corbis: Visuals Unlimited / Gary Meszaros (tc/Butterfly).
Dreamstime.com: Kaarsten (tc/torn paper).
Jacket images: Back: Corbis: Minden Pictures / Mark Moffett cla;
Spine: Corbis: Visuals Unlimited / Gary Meszaros
All other images © Dorling Kindersley Limited
For further information see: www.dkimages.com

Discover more at
www.dk.com

DK READERS

Bugs
Hide and Seek
Written by Laura Buller

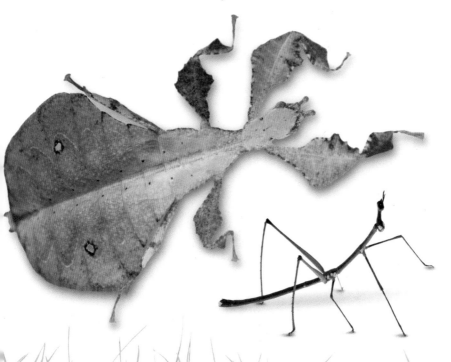

Psssst!

Hey, you!

Yes, you—the reader.

Can you find me?

Look up close.

Do you see me yet?

I know what you are thinking.

branch

Where am I hiding?
All you can see is
a tree branch.
Maybe I will hop down.
You are in for a big surprise!
Are you ready?

Ta dah!

Here I am.

Are you surprised?

leaf

I am not a leaf
fallen from the tree.
I am a bug.
I am called a walking leaf.
(Cool, right?)
My body looks just like
a real leaf.
That is how I can hide
in the trees.
I even move like a leaf.
I shake back and forth
like a leaf in the wind.

Looking like a leaf is helpful.
I can hide from other animals
that might want to eat me!
They can't tell me
from the leaves.
So they leave me alone!
I am not the only bug
that is good at hiding.

There are many bugs that
use this trick.
Would you like to meet
the others?
I warn you—some are
very hard to find!
Let's look for them.

Take a look!

Can you find anything
along the branch?
The branch is home
to a very smart bug.
Do you see it yet?

Look carefully
at the green twig.
It seems to have six legs!
That is not a twig.
It is a stick insect.

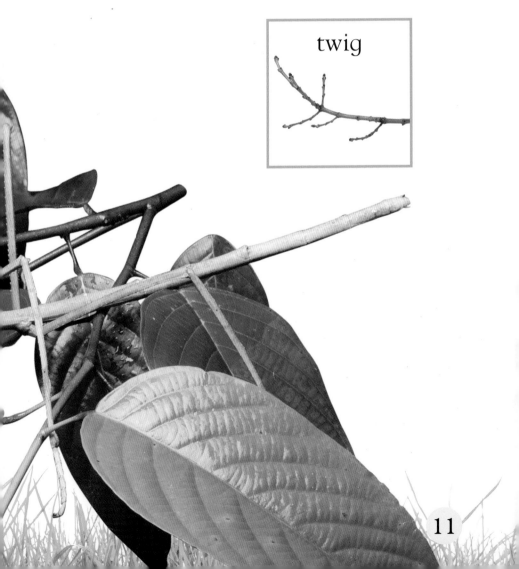

twig

The stick insect's body
is the same shape as a twig.
It is the same color, too.
A stick insect can stay
very still for ages.
It hides in the tree
all day long.

At night, the stick insect
hunts for food to eat.
It nibbles on tree leaves.
No one can see it
in the darkness.

By morning, the stick
insect is hiding again.
Let's not stick around!

Some plants are very green,
but there is much
more to be seen!
Look at this blade of grass.
Can you see a bright
green grasshopper?
The grasshopper is exactly
the same color as its home.
It blends in so well,
no one can see it—
apart from you, that is!
Now, let's get hopping.

blade of
grass

Look at this tree.
Its bark is so wrinkly
and brown.
This is not a good
hiding place for a bug.
Or is it?

Aha!

There is a cicada [si-KAY-da] hiding right on the tree. Its colors match the bark so well. Birds like to eat these bugs. The cicada stays very still until the bird flies past.

Be careful!

Do not prick your finger
on that thorny branch.
Those thorns look sharp.

Wait a second!
Those are not thorns.
They are treehoppers.

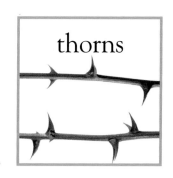

thorns

These bugs poke holes in
branches and feed on sap.
They can hide
and snack!
That is smart.

What do you see here?
A pile of rocks!
Maybe there is a bug
hiding there?

Wait a minute!
One of those rocks just moved.
I saw it with my own eyes!
That, my friend, is a rock bug.
A rock bug sits
as still as stone.

rock

What do we have here?
Something has landed
in the sand.
It is a grasshopper.
Its body colors match
the sandy grains.

Imagine you are a bird
flying over the beach.
Could you see that bug
in the sand?
I do not think so.
You would keep flying, and
miss out on your beach picnic.

What a strange-looking
bug we have here!
It is a spiny katydid.
This creature lives
in the rain forests.

Those thorns on its body
help it to hide in the forest.
Bats like to eat katydids,
but all those thorns can
scare them away.
(They are scaring me, too!)

I see a snake. Do you?
Hold on!
There is something odd
about that snake.
It is really a caterpillar,
playing a cool trick.

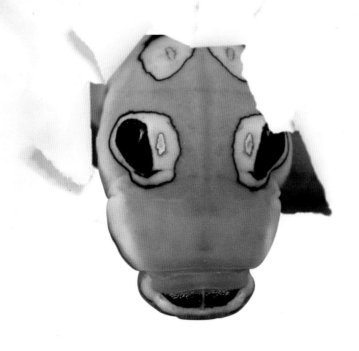

First it pulls in its legs.
Then it blows up
the front part of its body
like a balloon.
Spots on its underside look
just like snake's eyes.
Any bird who sees it
is sssssscared.

Wait a minute!

That bug reminds me
of someone.
Someone very close to me.
Someone who looks as if
it fell out of my family tree.

Bingo!

It's another leaf insect,
like me.
It's time for us to leave you.
We are off to a new
hiding place.
I wonder if you will
find us there.
We will see you.
Will you see us?
Keep looking!

Bugs Word Search

Some bugs look like other things.
Can you find these six hidden words?

bark   leaf   rock
sand   thorn   twig

t	h	o	r	n
w	s	r	o	b
i	l	n	c	a
g	e	g	k	r
s	a	n	d	k
k	f	e	a	d

Index

Word Search

t	h	o	r	n
w	s	r	o	b
i	l	n	c	a
g	e	g	k	r
s	a	n	d	k
k	f	e	a	d

DK READERS help children learn to read, then read to learn. If you enjoyed this DK READER, then look out for these other titles for your child.

Level 1 Deadly Dinosaurs
Roar! Thud! Meet Rexy, Sid, Deano, and Sonia, the dinosaurs that come alive at night in the museum. Who do you think is the deadliest?

Level 1 Little Dolphin
Follow Little Dolphin's adventures when he leaves his mother and joins the older dolphins for the first time. Will he be strong enough to keep up?

Level 1 Playful Puppy
Holly's dream has come true—she's been given her very own puppy. Share her delight in the playfulness of her new puppy as she tries to train him.

Level 1 Mega Machines
Hard hats on! The mega machines are very busy building a new school. Watch them in action!

Level 1 Pirate Attack!
Come and join Captain Blackbeard and his pirate crew for an action-packed adventure on the high seas.